Infinity Diary

THE PRIDE LIST

THE PRIDE LIST

EDITED BY SANDIP ROY AND BISHAN SAMADDAR

The Pride List presents new as well as classic works of
queer literature to the world. An eclectic collection of
books of queer stories, biographies, histories, thoughts,
ideas, experiences and explorations, the Pride List does
not focus on any specific region, nor on any specific
genre, but celebrates the fantastic diversity of LGBTQ+
lives across countries, languages, centuries and identi-
ties, with the conviction that queer pride comes from
its unabashed expression.

ALSO AVAILABLE FROM THE PRIDE LIST

MIREILLE BEST
Camille in October
Translated by Stephanie Schechner

MU CAO
In the Face of Death We Are Equal
Translated by Scott E. Myers

PAWAN DHALL
Out of Line and Offline:
Queer Mobilizations in '90s Eastern India

CYRIL WONG

Infinity Diary

Seagull BOOKS

LONDON NEW YORK CALCUTTA

Seagull Books, 2020

© Cyril Wong, 2020

ISBN 978 0 8574 2 742 7

British Library Cataloguing-in-Publication Data
A catalogue record for this book is available from the British Library

Book designed by Bishan Samaddar, Seagull Books, Calcutta, India, using line drawings by Alice Attie and Mahmud Husain Laskar; images courtesy the artists.

Printed and bound by WordsWorth India, New Delhi, India

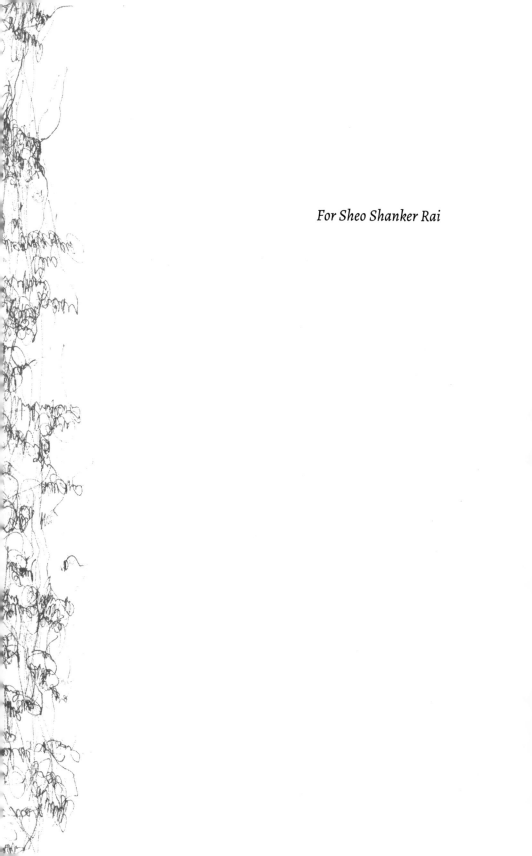

For Sheo Shanker Rai

Contents

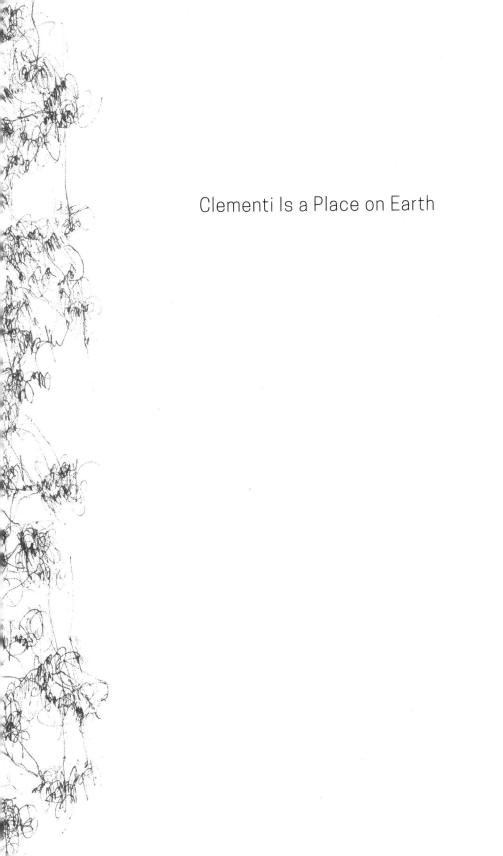

Clementi Is a Place on Earth

Every morning, old ladies tread carefully between their flats and the market, keeping death from spilling from their bodies.

Another new cleaner who clears my plate says thank you when I say thank you.

Tissue-paper girls screech when crows part their wings, accurately missing their faces.

Regular guy in a striped shirt balances his face, keeping his smile in check in case he looks crazy.

That noodle-shop couple is unhappy all the time—aren't you glad we're nothing like them?

All comparisons are deceitful; I'm the fly on the amputated limb of a cigarette butt sliding off the top of that rubbish bin.

Beauty is every story we dream up about God and the Universe, or these plates of food arranged by colour at the Indian Muslim stall; creation, just creation, is something else altogether different— brown tea in my glass cup whose transparency hides nothing you don't already know.

The Clementi Mall is a manic tragedy. Nobody slows down. Then there are empty corridors along the outside of the building on the higher floors where you may take in an elevated view of the void.

Am I the only one who dares to solve these tangram heartland corridors of no-time?

An absurd, elderly gentleman jogs with a walker and lunges face-first into the pavement when anyone hovers too close alongside.

Millennials bloat their novels and jostle for international agents while Cikgu Latiff, a poet, sits here at his usual corner in the unrenovated coffee shop, wondering if anybody recognizes him.

How many still think we'll learn the meaning of our suffering in newspapers delivered to our flats in heaven? Imagine us queueing before some ATM in the hereafter, as if for the currency of insight; or for lottery numbers inside the NTUC, long after it has been torn down—waiting for nothing.

Most of us are sponge cake—sold here at Avenue Two's only confectionery: neither harmless nor unhealthy, unless you believe the news that all cakes are dangerous. But intention is everything, many would urge; not like ice cream or soft drinks that hasten diabetes, even cancer. In a way, some might say, all life is sponge cake.

I'm a poet of intangible things, so my audience doesn't quite exist; their absence is the glare from the newly minted pavement under the unbearable sun where the playground was demolished.

Metal cylinder under a tree; metal cylinder is me post-language,
rusting nonetheless and heavy with ash.

Sitting with a migrant worker near the Central Food Centre, I hear
about a possible marriage in the future, arranged by his father, and
books of poems he plans to publish back home in Bengali (writing is
already his wife, I tell him). I cannot stop looking too long into his
eyes: Would his irises still be wet with grasping and swirling with
restlessness when he's fifty? Do we ever settle and why not?

The uncle at my table utilizes the last of his testosterone protesting
loudly to two other uncles before him who pat themselves secretly on
the thigh for not being like him. In a neighbourhood in the next
galaxy, as the poet Ruth Stone once suggested, there would be nothing
to complain about; even the mynah scooping crumbs off the floor
would realize time is an absurd hotel. (There, we'd still hold hands
and die in our sleep; no cancers, stroke or punishing dementia.)

Only on Sundays does Avenue Two mimic the purlieu of the MRT, or
the rest of the island; this island of 'I'm tired and so what if I collide
into you on my way home, old man'; island of 'Look at this Chinese
boy still sitting at our usual table, thinking we don't mind sharing it
with him; look at him reading his phone and pretending not to care
as we talk loudly in a language he never bothered to learn'; of panic
and never-enough and nobody-really-cares-about-each-other-so-
why-should-I.

I keep returning to that dead bird on the train platform at peak hour,
its comma head snug against its own unheaving chest.

A guy in an exercise singlet is recognized by every hawker, so nobody really notices when he sings every morning at the top of his voice. When he sees that a dazed, older man having breakfast is unaware of blood flowing from a cut above the eyebrow, he whips out a tissue and holds it against the man's brow until the bleeding stops. He also pays for the man's meal. There are arhats among us that we never acknowledge; not that they need to be.

My *anandamaya kosha* reverberated like a plucked string throughout the sheaths of my body on my way back to Clementi station on a silent train. This music at the heart of all potentiality didn't last, nor did I expect it to. Every *kosha* or layer of being builds towards a structure like the surface of a balloon; the air within is neither bliss nor annihilation. It's beyond our discussion of it, if you can imagine that.

An effeminate fellow with long, vibrating, curly hair pushes past slower pedestrians to get ahead with one hand like a gnarled antenna raised to the sky. You might say he looks like me when I'm madder than mad (you'd say this lovingly, of course) or like any number of artists in this country, except artists are better equipped to hide their desire to win. I like how others look at him first with contempt, then forgiveness, when they can tell he's mad.

Flux of bodies, flux of thought and feeling, flux of flux within flux along every floor—the mall a manic tragedy I could stand in the middle of and cry and laugh with everybody looking, but I don't.

Thought doesn't even begin to sink its teeth into the surface of things and yet we reside in its mouth. If you sold your car, we could take the train together to Jurong East past the fire station, beside which a golden Buddha sits on the roof of a temple, beyond caring or not caring, beyond thought and time and for all time.

The West Coast temple is haunted, I swear. It uses white toilet tiles for its walls, which is in keeping with what I thought about religion: a toilet we shit in and which flushes our shit back down our gullets.

A father—or maybe the grandfather—carries a toddler down the stairs to the hardware shops. You always exclaim how cute he is—the child, not the man—but I can only see what he'll look like in his dotage.

A cough discharges a glob of saliva on the table to which tiny, brown ants are soon drawn, drinking what was once inside my mouth—what sweetness could I possibly possess and why not sip from puddles on pavements everywhere else in-between bouts of rain? The sky overhead rattles like a chain.

Another void-deck funeral, another day; another void-deck wedding, another day.

Avenue Two is slower than other parts of Clementi; I'm not being metaphorical. Maybe it's all in my head. But I'm grateful for its slowness; for conditions that help to diminish my mental tendencies. When I'm here (and not just because I get to wake up with you), my mind is almost a stilled harp.

I saw that jogger with his walker again today. The skin around his right eye was purple and swollen. One day, another fall will kill him. If I didn't live in this neighbourhood, I'd suspect abuse in his home. Imagine how many must have told him he shouldn't be running. Imagine not knowing how to listen.

Neighbours picking up shit after their dogs; neighbours forgetting to pick up their shit.

A publisher asked me to write a love letter to the residents of my neighbourhood. After I submitted my piece, I'm told to edit it so it might sound gentler and more compassionate towards the end.

Now the noodle shop is run solely by the wife.

Nobody or no body is the same. No thought (its convoy of emotions, trailing behind) or place, either. Like how that laundry shop has been reduced to an automated DIY counter. I took a photograph of you depositing clothes at the older shop and turning to search for me. I remember thinking this is how one begins on a journey, you leaving your clothes behind. Was our time in Clementi the start of everything or the beginning of the end? Your face so white in that image, a glowing candle—your whiteness a receding trace I wanted to store away.

Between You and Infinity

Outside the window
beyond our bed,
a woman downstairs
coughs, an older man
is laughing; even farther
this morning, a ship horn
blows its dim, dark note
that nobody else hears,
not even you.

I'm a small animal inside the cave
of your need. As if by some law
of physics, the contents of my head
stop shifting when I rest
against your arm. After a question,
'Because you're my baby'
becomes the only explanation
that matters.

A path through commas of hair
on your chest is a highway
to forever, but there're other paths
demanding to be travelled
alone, longer and more difficult,
the same destination in sight.
What happens when I stop
in the middle of such a path
and turn around to remember
you're no longer there?

I stand on your feet
like how you once stood
on your late father's feet
to dance. If I'm too heavy,
you say nothing, carrying me
in a foxtrot across an invisible
ballroom floor of time.

If the highest achievement
is also its opposite, then
there's nothing to be gained
from winning the lottery
or placing your hand on my face.
In moments when desire recedes
and affection for you glows as if
from a distance, my body is an island
of unbearable peace.

Doubt is my best friend,
my truest certainty, the master
of impermanence and 'I told you so';
who sings sweet nothings
in my ear every morning and epic
lullabies till I sleep. You're the reason
I neglect her. But when you're at work,
we meet for coffee. We watch
television together and listen to songs
that destroy us in happy ways.
I don't expect you to like her,
as she cares little about you too.

You and infinity:
lovers I get caught
in-between. Waking
to your kiss reminds
me again that both
are the same. And how
without one, I'm still
left with the other.

My mother told her children we must
never marry anyone outside our race,
never leave the church,
never become queer. I've never
been more Chinese, more holy, more
conventional than when I'm with you,
my lovely Indian man.
Your Hindu sacred thread moves
against my skin like a shifting line
in sand. When my wrist gets caught
in its loop, I know we're conjoined and
already blessed.

Has every path led to you
or is it *through*—
Every day is a struggle,
it's true. We're losing
each other as we speak.
Existence isn't a road
but an avalanche
in slow motion.

'Let's say farewell now,
so we won't have to say it
when the stars claim us.'

I love you
as much as I love
my kidneys; as I love
to breathe; to make you
frown with mock displeasure;
to tease and appease;
to know when I repeat,
'I love you,' it remains
the only explanation
that matters.

In a dream, I was all of me
in a parallel life. Upon waking,
I'm reminded that I can't be
anyone else; your body
is proof. Yet I can still be
uncertain. Touching, sighing.
Lies needn't be the truth.
We're mirrors and everybody
the same. A new morning,
I nearly believe this.

As a poet, I'm accustomed
to small audiences.
As a reader, only poems
incite insight.
As a lover, tiny frictions
excite me.
As a city dweller, tight spaces
are home.
As your partner, just a glance
takes for ever.

Dreaming of Kyoto in Osaka
and growing old in that town
where shrines would knock
tranquility into us at every turn
and a Buddha statue is composed
from ashes of the dead.
But food would hold no flavour
for your curried tongue; ryokans
have no proper chairs and the floor
is not for sleeping. A distant mountain
we'd never climb together
reminds me of our bodies
melded peacefully on a funeral pyre.

We think about moving to Malaysia
when we have enough money
or when we run out of excuses.
Anywhere freer than Singapore.
Not freer, but across the causeway
we could disappear in that hinterland
that isn't an island; that is vast enough.
We talk of leaving but never go.
Night inclines us to each other.
Two homosexuals in a possibly more
conservative country—the irony.
Or maybe not at all ironic, since
being invisible is what we're used to
and now it could be an advantage.
Yes, the irony. No hope of changing
society; instead we pick a Malaccan
condo beside a hospital, as healthcare
is important in our old age. Imagine
that: we might die together
far from here, when our home here
shades into a dream we might finally
depart, before waking up together
inside a better dream. *Our merging*
bodies on the bed; peninsula
withstanding the sea.

I confessed to Bette Midler tearily
in a dream that I loved the song
'The Glory of Love' from *Beaches*:
how it took me off from having to be
anything more than a listener in love.
I think I cried because it wasn't just
for me that I was sad, but for everyone
forgotten and alone. I woke up
without tears because I realized
we're not fragments; we don't need
to be somebody—lover, winner—
to be whole. *I'm nobody with a name*
and lighter than air. So easy
for me to say this, I know,
since I get to wake up in your arms.

This afternoon I danced
with my younger self. We danced
to Adele's 'Water under the Bridge'
because. Just because. Crows of
loneliness leaving our shoulders
when we whirled, embracing. And you
weren't there. (Do you mind?
Can you still love us; I mean, me?)
We healed each other. The world
could fuck itself. I'm writing
to restage our little number. So you
may watch us disappear into me.

When the mind moves faster
than light and so it freezes—
our marriage plays out in multiple
scenes on a distant screen;
forming, deforming, un-
forming. Until the return to where
we are now, like a rubber band
springing back to its original shape.
What am I left with that I'm left
to continue? What keeps me going
except for the slow hand of time
and the minutiae of love?

Beyond the grandest university
of solitude and emptiness,
there are only rituals of survival
and the heart's minute longings
for the pillow of your abdomen,
frayed carpet of your chest,
ear hairs I trim to keep you young
and your inner child that jumps out
when my inner parent arises.
Two worlds in my body orbiting
each other without collision; laws
of space, time and gravity
still holding everything in check.

Every path traversed, the way
every place, the quiet collapse
of a multiverse, buildings
shuddering when they
have never stirred before,
shivering to a different standstill,
park benches arching like cats
then settling into benches.
What has faltered
is the belief that nothing
has altered. In medias res,
that story has begun
to be recanted.

I'm back. You're here too.
A ship horn blows its dim, dark
note. We carry on.

A construction worker wishes there was less
sun. I read in a magazine that some actor
is pissed because he didn't win a prize.
I'd like this poem to gather more levels
of meaning, more of what I feel about you
in it. Another bird believes it can go higher,
and does. 'Is that a crow?' you ask.
I wish I could say *Yes*, so you'd smile,
knowing you've been right.

At last, the mind has stopped
swinging from room to room
of thought, no longer hurting itself
banging into hardened opinions
like random furniture. I can't talk
to anyone who doesn't understand—
but you do, you do. Placing
your forehead upside down on mine
and staying there, just staying there
so both of us might rest.

How many at Italy's anti-gay rally
must also hate ISIS, thus missing
the boat of irony completely.
(Look: Muslims and Christians getting
along, at last, or just briefly.)
This reminder that after dispersing
the hatred, a love like ours sits calmly
at the bloodied centre. Avoiding
the insanely religious, the religiously
insane, those incapable of drawing
away the veils of time and certainty—
is also learning the art of being
alone, on our pathless road to clarity.

Who made the Maker?
If He makes the mountain
immovable, can He move it?
(Could you prove it?)
Perfect and all-powerful or not;
then why and why not:
questions without reasonable
answers, their absurdity
watering the roots of religious
contempt for our kind.
So make a boat of ourselves
and we might sail the shame.
You, my temple; I, your cathedral.
Let not the divine divide us
but make us already the same.

When we love like this,
we're all the broken boys and
our own religion.

Wait, what was the problem
that has been solved? How to live
without a lover's touch
and is leaving without leaving you
too much? A part
is no longer apart, I know,
yet here we are, our gazes
still forming a tunnel
between nowhere and everywhere.

'Hinduism has an answer
for everything,' you assured me,
'and for everyone, even atheists.'
'All roads go to Orchard Road,
all rivers to the same sea,'
you once joked to a young monk
and lousy listener. Moksha
is nirvana is infinity I grazed
by chance on a train to nowhere,
later making that rookie mistake
of hunting again for that which
never needed to be found.

Why I'm not a serious Buddhist
is because attachment must be enjoyed
and run its course, I've discovered.
Your smell on the pillow:
there one moment, memory
the next, releasing it soon after—
the agony not so much unbearable
but a part of me that I carry
for now in a raft of these words.

I'm a man inside a cave
inside another cave, more intent
to gaze between my toes
than make art or lament
about impermanence. But I should
explain myself. So I'm
writing this for you. Longing
is exhausting, appearing
as a tray of cheesecake
riding a rising tide of shit.
I still like cheesecake
and sometimes I taste shit.
It doesn't matter: I carry on,
finishing a life I never started.
I carry on.

Living is
dying is loving
us for now.

I'll learn to let go
when I learn to let go;
calling your name
in your absence, then
losing the wish to call;
an ice cube held for
so long it melts
nonetheless in my fist.

Clear the decks:
no more you or me.
Alertness.

A ship or foghorn
I misheard?
The sea is still there.

For at least a minute
at dawn when our bed
is missing you, I ask,
What story is this?
Other times: *Why am I*
back here? Always
in the midst of waiting
for a hundred shoes
to drop. I half-forgot
those trees with yellow
flowers outside, basking
as if from insight; that old
man downstairs whose laugh
has become my alarm
clock. I pretend that this
is still my story to tell.

When love has nothing
to do with that overrated
metaphor, the heart—
stab, burst and forget it—
but everything to do with
the mind; the mind
all windows, an open door;
step inside from out
under that ridiculous sun,
dear lover, friend
or enemy: you can
stay only briefly; time
ushering every presence
out of me, sprucing up
after, leaving little trace;
the mind not a house now
but its own metaphor,
synecdoche or metonymy;
a part or reflection
of the whole (who can say
and why the compulsion
to spell it out anyway?)

Rest against the need for rest.
All is nothing is lost. I wake up
from a dream in which a friend
was arrested for taking drugs
and she wrote a poem about how
all of us are stars. I wake up to you
telling me to discard your ashes
at Changi beach; I reply that I'd
eat them instead. What abides
is knowing every permutation
of reality is reality for somebody.
The self is overrated but since
we're tossed in this reality, I exist
and cannot rest. Nothing is lost,
that's all, despite the apparent
non sequitur. You're in the living
room writing an essay on religion
while rain grazes the windows.
I'm resting and cannot rest.

I think I should have learnt
years ago in that writers' tent
at Edinburgh, waiting for
Susan Sontag to get off
the computer so I could send
an email home; observing her
as she mocked the festival director
for getting her biography wrong;
that first instant I might have
begun to undo the knot of labels
like 'artist' or 'poet' within
myself. Later, when I joke
to a student that I'm 'a house-
wife that happens to write,'
the mind has become lighter
than when I'd fought to be heard.
Now, as I wait for you to appear
at our door, my eyes have been
shut for a time, no palisades
of selfhood to fracture
vision—then your face appears
and a love I cannot relinquish
weighs down the space that's left.

Nothing taken seriously
and seriously taken. Tender
iris, the moon makes no enemies.
Walls link arms for each other.
Inside an asylum, one might
still be sane and listening.
You're my second sight
through which I'm shimmering.
Time grinds hard but time
doesn't keep score.
Wakefulness is a bed: let's recline
before it's over. I'm yours.

Love isn't for everyone. Wanting
to exit is a lifelong addiction.
Just because we know the words
it doesn't mean we *know*.
You and I must live alongside
crazies and monsters; your skin
is armour I learn to wear over mine.
I write this as a mnemonic
for sanity. Forever is a number
we sing together but in different keys.
Oneness is an embrace that chimes
for now. Between waiting for you
and a wish to leave, clouds gather
to create a dragon or a rip in time.
Other people is other people
but watchfulness and potentiality
reside behind every story of a life.
Love showed up once we surrendered.
Let's do the same for infinity.

The mind is an unbroken glass
of water in which every thought
or feeling spreads like spilt
ink, until all the water
is a singular colour: dark
or light. Don't forget the water
is both cloudy and clear.
Don't forget about the glass.

What words in their best order
might swing the mind from attachment;
stopping the rerun of thought,
emotions standing like a dazed audience
to leave an empty cinema?
What words to repel words
that crowd the heart, leaving
no room for wonder?
Is this the responsibility of philosophy
or poetry, since religion has failed me?
If along corridors of language,
the avoidance of every door
becomes the beginning of intelligence.
A smile and a nod while I walk
away from inside the self—
Bow to words, they carried us
so far; any further
you must do it on your own.

Travelling Light

The meditator moves from room to room, but his lover is everywhere.

If we heard what everyone was thinking, we might choose to stop thinking altogether.

The unknown rang the doorbell, bearing gifts of knives and air.

✳

Creation is the mirror in which we surrender.

What we make gives us form, then swells beyond us—like love.

Before holocausts in every direction, what first whirls before the creator?

✳

The mind keeps waiting to land; a tennis ball violently served.

Before my head was cleared, I had a vision of you walking away.

Soon I receded too, our bedroom like a womb I was leaving for another birth; time peeling off me like a glove.

✳

What body behind this body of appetite, conditioned ticks and taunts, kicking to stay?

The embodied mind beyond everything else; a pillow you still sometimes rest against.

Then when your head is lifted: a clearing at the start of another infinite day.

✳

Rapunzel in a watchtower of restive meat; a refugee behind a rusty chain-link fence.

Consciousness like a corridor of doors opening and closing to all my senses in a house already burning to the ground.

Every door gone, flesh as smouldering rubble: Do I search for you in the wide expanse?

✳

Swimming past the bedrock of every argument until thinking becomes the problem to be found.

The majority of us fidget in fear between not thinking and never thinking deeply enough—the language of deception dangles a middle path.

Birds after the rain make a melancholy sound.

✳

No words or analysis, thus no doubt and apprehension about change: a laugh in the present is just a laugh.

I still miss you when you're not here, that's all.

What we are is all I may ever know of love, but even now the thought of us blends into a requiem of clouds like a dove—it's enough.

*

Don't try—to try is never to do it—but drop the ball of thinking completely and refuse to examine its fall.

The instant as variation, open to revision; in a dream, I had looked up a French noun that meant 'unmoving' and 'absolute', which didn't exist upon waking.

Past tense as a bubbled vesicle or caul.

*

Which movie or novel isn't about the suffering and consequences of judgement and thought, and why don't we simply make friends with the solitariness of being?

No afterthought, after thought, the purity of every action in reaction and the unburdened release of that action.

No house of whipping wings on one's back: we kiss just once, but I'm lighter upon departing.

✳

A touch to second touch, first dance to last, but when I don't touch, don't dance, breathing analysed to its smallest fraction.

Remember to write to remember to forget: no more mantra like the gripping of reins to restrain impermanence; the choice of choicelessness taking over what's left of me.

Death's scissoring beyond every aftereffect of any option, the acknowledgement of the rules of change ensuring a slow peristalsis of desire, a defecation.

✳

Our dreams still so small, so full of unfinished business: a poem, your laundry turning over itself with difficulty in the wash; what we complete—like our embrace—dwindling swiftly.

Sit down, do nothing, a lighthouse penetrating soundlessly across every dream and lifetime.

Your face in my hands: the way your eyes close is always too pretty.

✳

Singing to a song on the radio is surfing a current of remembered hurt and arriving on sand, absurdly bone-dry; a grin across my face like a path a fugitive cuts fleeing a crime.

The fact that every thought at best remains a lucky guess: would we always love each other—*yes*—and even after one of us is absent— *yes*—

Whatever happens, we extend each other, or one continues from where the other left off—to know this without thought, without effort of analysis—like reverberations after a story's last line.

✳

Who doesn't feel as if there's no choice in the matter, and we only did our best?

Who doesn't believe that there can be no other way, from Jesus to the Buddha?

Who doesn't have faith that trees hide their faces from sunlight like vampires reluctant to be blessed?

✳

'What's the point of anything when every view is permissible?' asked the laughing bodhisattva.

Neither wrong nor right, certain nor uncertain, when every side you take can be flipped like a table or a coin.

With nothing left to confuse us, nothing left to do but love, doubt exposed and time's conditioning arrested, we've come so far.

✳

Sometimes I think we're extreme funnels of a vaster, insurmountable energy; the self a further tightening, like an addiction; the amnesia regarding infinity to which we remain conjoined.

Slipstreams sideways, seductive side doors opening to rooms that begin to narrow like one another, before you know it you're sloping towards forgetting that vortices may be unwound—why not relinquish our tornadoes?

I was in a dream about forever before you called me back (the dream still expanding madly inside me) with a kiss to the groin.

*

I've an idea about what the world should be, so do you; to agree, one must persuade the other; or to win, one must die or kill the other; underlying the idea is the possibility of the idea—How to live with possibility alone without leaving it for the hell that follows?

How we've done it, keeping beliefs out of the bedroom: cocooned in potential, silence what our bodies accrue.

Without the signifiers for time and change and the wish to make you understand them, are we no longer divided: from the lips of Whitney Houston, 'How will I know—?'

*

If awareness without selfhood or motive is the same—an empty coracle bobbing on a lake inside a caldera—for each of us, why am I still explaining myself to you?

Gross to subtle, atman or the subtlest—smaller than mustard seeds, more distant than stars—what remains to be accumulated?

Let's play that game of matryoshka dolls; arrive at the tiniest one then open that to find me there too.

✸

A lesson in expectation the length of a life—or a lie, which lasts only as long as expected.

This scene in which our hands (look at them) are already interlocked, as we cross the shared stream of our minds on foot together—What if one of us looked back, would either of us dare?

The lover moves from room to room, but the meditator is everywhere waiting to be discovered.

Infinity Diary

What lightning in a metal bowl of water collected by the window?
A thunderstorm in the chest falls mostly on deaf ears. How to tell
you I still wish I didn't have to wake up every morning? What's that
line by Sexton again about carpenters, 'they want to know *which
tools . . . never why build?*' It's true. It's true. Not from the usual
reasons like despair or a haughty resignation, no, but a desiccation,
a surrendering to nothingness like the closing of a book. What
keeps me

*dusty shoe cabinet, hairs in the drainhole, unkept underwear, a giggle when
my cheek grazes your stomach*

going is the unfinished business of chores, your face through the
door in the evening, that kind of thing. Then there are others:
a companion who is going blind and who once threatened to leave
because he was terrified of hurting me; or one who loves me for the
way I listen and speak when he listens; and another who used to be
my best friend but is quietly packing away our history in boxes and
moving away. We carry on.

*rusty refrigerator magnets, slippers pointing in disparate directions, floor
mat slightly askew, bulb of your shoulder in the mirror*

What stirred the first archaea in deep oceanic vents or along the
sensuous flanks of volcanoes? What is movement, this wish for

more? I don't want more. Not that I'm obsessed with your depar-
ture, but you're my synecdoche, a symptom of everything I hoped
would leave me alone to live a full death, commence my letting go.
Without you, I mean, I can really go.

*gentle foghorn still blows in the distance, the old ladies' qigong group down-
stairs is dwindling so maybe most of them are dead, some days there're just
no letters in the mailbox*

What scares me is this spiralling towards a simplicity nearly
impossible to resist, in the direction of full knowledge that every
colour belongs to the same swirly dress of light; that every value or
objection reflects one another; living is dying is arising again in
different form; while all that's left is what we do to each other and
then we're done. What scares me is that with acceptance, I won't be
able to grieve for long: the sweetness of rowing along a wound's
unending channel; your face like a claw wedged into every limb so
every gesture must hurt of you after you're gone. Do you fear

*shirts that disappear from the cupboard and the laundry basket, insects
mistaken for cockroaches huddling in corners of the flat and dying there,
speaking wind chimes, crestfallen blanket on the floor*

the same thing? Clouds smash their light bulbs against every win-
dow. Wind is a sentence of breath that began in the lungs of another
universe, syllables mocking us now with indecipherable meaning,
full of praise and warning. Then rain like a symphonic language all
of its own, importunate and haranguing. Something apophatic
when a stillness stands up inside me to take notice of inclement

weather and reminds me of what it isn't; what can be negated without dismissal, like dancing on a bridge in the middle of a typhoon.

shirt draping the couch like a discarded white flag, lust-red pillows, water stains on the table from a weeping cup of ice

Symmetries our bodies align with for pleasure, conditionings of beauty, drawing and redrawing every impulse to belong and disappear, fucking strangers or rearrangements of furniture—no real difference in outcome, the older we become—before we fill up the body completely; I mean, fill it to the brim as breath tapers and the heart is no longer a metaphor; self and the body one and the same punctuation in time, a fallen brick or dense fog shimmering so brightly it's no longer separate from the light that fills it like an awareness of itself

washed pot not yet returned to the cupboard, beads of rice on the stove, gambolling ball of tissue

or a permanent forgetting. The second law of thermodynamics is the reason many believe time exists, moving forward not back: you can't unmix coffee, blood cannot be adjured to abjure its viruses, entropy or disorder the order of the day; when fog becomes light and the light no longer divisible—but maybe this is time moving backward too, first forward then back, from clear to unclear to clarified constituents, or one singular constituent; before dividing again, becoming

drops of water on the table and the floor you think make the kitchen unclean,
you scold me for not cleaning up

unclear, conflicted, colliding, converging; conditioned, born again:
miasma, haze, fog, smog. I'm struggling to see the point of living,
even now. Not even our bodies purling around each other in the
reluctant light of evening can persuade me to forget the struggle:
the struggle to talk, move, read; even as I somehow talk, move, read,
even write. The point of the struggle is that it never goes away, even
as I'm sitting here, not looking like I'm surrendering to any type of
struggle at all. Maybe I've chosen the wrong word. Maybe the word

the empty fragrance of clean office shirts that I must fold to fit your suitcase
as you prepare to go to India for two weeks, the blackness of your work pants

is weariness. Even the rain conspires to make me forget you, beating
the windows and blowing its many trumpets. Life is longer than any
longing. It's what I've heard and now I'm told. If nothing lasts, it's
nothing I'll return to, my farthest sanctum or highest castle; if the
subtlest mind doesn't last, then it doesn't even matter. Two things I
strive not to forget: the throb of love and the unceasing fact of its
possibility—how separate, but also the same.

video CDs with lewd topless men on the covers, left in your drawer from the
nineties, making me laugh instead of turning me on

In porn, the actors never go home afterwards to talk universe,
Hindu gods, your overprotective sisters, office politics. Beauty is
skin on muscle over bone is still beauty, nonetheless, that sucks us

70

in because we let it. Your late father came to Singapore from India on a train then a boat with barely enough money in his pocket for a dream—I suddenly think of him and your mother as ghosts peering in through the rain we never saw coming; marvelling at your silver altar in the living hall; looking at each other as I lift your shirt to fondle your chest.

tiny metal scissors left beside the tissue-box for curtailing hairs swimming out of your ears

We are not separate from the movement of desire; no *we* distinct from want, which has never been a door waiting to be opened but wheels within wheels; such grinding music of uncelestial spheres; each moment we demand transcendence, wheels wheel faster, harder, more efficiently, when the *I* is already desire, wanting—for truth is something else; not separate, not any sparrow floating over a roof, but part of the warp and woof that might untighten; every wheel slowly slowing, winding down, given a chance.

framed pictures of your late parents on the shelf, you holding a friend's baby in your arms, two of us standing and grinning in front of a public statue I don't recognize with your arm like a bracket over my shoulder

Stopped rain only promises future rain. Then it's here before we know it; we didn't even hear it invade our periphery. After the fierce gossip of thought, bodies worn down and worn out, what is left: seeing without waiting, a touch losing its demands; words are houses for married silences. In a spontaneous picture of ourselves captured on my phone, your dazzling mezzaluna smile makes up for my closed mouth, which is further hidden behind my fist, so only my eyes are dominant, squinting as if I'm already foretelling the end of everything that I'd ever need to say.

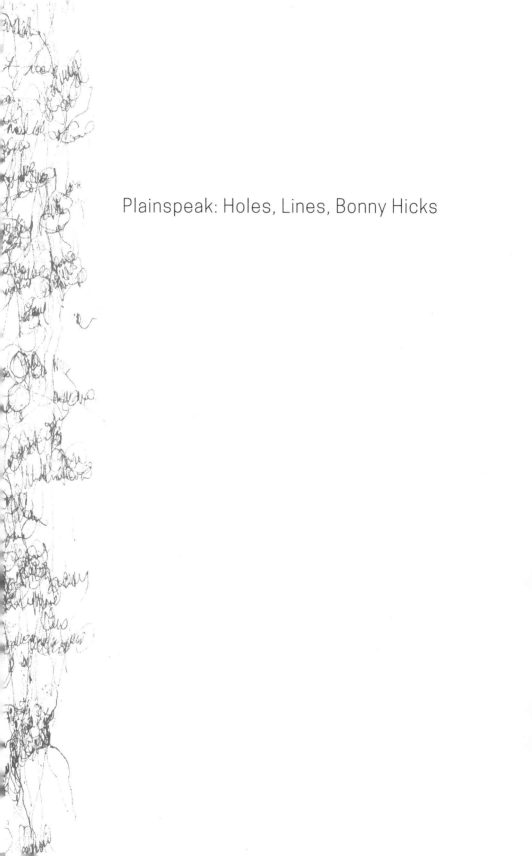

Plainspeak: Holes, Lines, Bonny Hicks

Whether we know it or not, we still wait for each other to go.

Every morning, another sentence appears in my head; I believe these lines add up to a story.

Nothing tallies.

We never stop trying to become what others told us we cannot be.

Everyone carries on, unjust or not.

Always something that fills the mind before anticipation; before knowing how long it remains there.

Just because you see a hole, you keep wanting to fill it.

I want to love with greater openness, but I grow suspicious and strange.

People seldom care as much as they like to.

Limited perspectives aside, everything is a surprise.

Can you guess the exact moment of your childhood that made you what you are today?

We remain the sum of what we were, even when we forget.

Narratives aren't the full story; something is always left out.

You told me you were sexually molested as a child in a cinema; *Pete's Dragon* was playing and it was the year I was born.

Tragic synchronicities are only funny to me.

Present tense is future perfect.

Everyone has opinions—all that noise.

Twenty years after the abuse took place, SilkAir Flight MI 185 crashed into a Sumatran river.

Before poets became more honest in writing about their own lives in Singapore, there was Bonny Hicks (who was killed on that plane).

Her fiancé died beside her. (Was she lucky or unlucky?)

She was a fashion model who wrote about topics (like sex) that made stupid Singaporeans uncomfortable.

She also wrote: *Health is merely the slowest possible rate at which one can die.*

Heaven can wait, but I cannot. I cannot take for granted that time is on my side.

I experienced great happiness and great sorrow in my life. While the great happiness was uplifting and renewing, the sorrow ate at me slowly, like a worm in the core of an apple.

The sorrow which I experienced was often due to the fact that my own happiness came at a price. That price was someone else's happiness.

Grace Chia eulogized Hicks in her poem, 'Mermaid Princess': . . . *spoke too soon / too loud / too much out of turn . . . / too much of I, I, I, I—* The government doesn't care about your feelings; just make sure you contribute to society.

I like what Bertrand Russell writes in 'In Praise of Idleness': . . . *a great deal of harm is being done in the modern world by belief in the virtuousness of work, and that the road to happiness and prosperity lies in an organized diminution of work.*

He defines work like this: . . . *of two kinds: first, altering the position of matter at or near the earth's surface relatively to other such matter; second, telling other people to do so. The first kind is unpleasant and ill paid; the second is pleasant and highly paid.*

Singaporean politicians are highly paid.

When I write, things become clear to me; when I seem random, I become even clearer.

I'm clearing matter from the surface of my mind.

On BBC News, the prime minister spoke about the law that criminalizes gay men in Singapore: *An uneasy compromise, I'm prepared to live with it . . .*

A friend and poet responded on Facebook: *WHAT THE FUCK DOES WHAT *YOU* ARE PREPARED TO LIVE WITH HAVE *ANYTHING* TO DO WITH ACTUAL GAY PEOPLE YOU WORTHLESS, SPINELESS OVERPAID SHITNUGGET OF AN AMOEBA.*

My favourite kind of homophobes are those that believe they aren't homophobic, by virtue of the fact that they feel 'sorry' or 'compassion' for us.

I can live with bullshit; bullshit never gave me much of a choice.

Religion teaches us to be grateful.

Fuck religion.

When there are no more thoughts in my head, it means I have no more 'you' in my head.

Another friend died today. Drugs and illness killed him. He took drugs because he was depressed. He didn't think he was depressed.

When society tells you what you are is wrong, this does something to you.

Somebody once close to me insisted that bad medical care was the main cause of his death. He won't accept my explanation.

Years before the drugs, my friend was plumper, gossipy and kind. We had late suppers together (oddly enough, at the University Hospital cafeteria; although it wasn't the same hospital where he died).

But it was in Manila (we were part of a choir that travelled abroad) where he came out to me, promising he didn't have a crush on me or anything like that.

He just needed me to know.

The conductor of the choir declined to attend his funeral. I didn't attend, either; I didn't want to meet other choir members who understood less about his life than I did.

Heaven can wait, but I cannot.

Living fills me with disappointment that I learnt to accept—even use.

The Cree have a word 'Aayahkwew' that translates as 'neither man nor woman'; the Navajo have 'nàdleehé' or 'one who changes'. But is there a word for 'genderless heart of ever-widening holes'?

My holes are merging into one.

Christian women rang our bell to evangelize after noticing a portrait of Hanuman hanging above our door.

You gave me a look that stopped me from cursing at them.

I love my anger and sorrow as much as my need to love.

If I become unfeeling, it still means I care, but differently.

Does this make you unhappy?

Bonny Hicks: *I think and feel, therefore I am.*

Poetry is not just the way I prefer to organize my thoughts; it has been my way of moving beyond thinking and feeling.

Hicks, again: *When we take embodied thinking rather than abstract reasoning as a goal for our mind, then we understand that thinking is a transformative act. The mind will not only deduce, speculate, and comprehend, but it will also awaken . . . and inspire.*

The Oddfellows, a Singaporean band I listened to, composed 'Your Smiling Face' for Hicks: *. . . another day of nothing; that everything is the same, if only I know your game, yeah everything is the same, I see the smile on your face . . .*

And if love is blind, then I can't see what you're hiding inside.

Sometimes I think I've misheard the lyric: *. . . if love is blind, I can see what you're hiding . . .*

I neither think of myself as good nor bad. I think only when vanishing down these lines.

To almost see the goodness you see in me.

Maybe I reflect parts of you that are good; like a mirror, not 'me' at all.

Then when you're gone—

Hicks (apocryphally): *How glorious it is to be good! I have discovered its secrets and I want to spread the word.*

Dear Stupid Straight People

Don't invite us to your housewarming where homophobia waits like a blind, rabid dog without a leash.

The animal is always in the guise of a god-loving person.

Don't tell me our suffering is the same, when I hear all about yours in the media and you've never deeply wondered about mine.

Don't tell us about your marital problems, when we can't even fuck without remembering that it's still a crime.

When more people than you can envision prefer that we didn't exist.

Don't tell me heaven has a plan, because this must mean your stupidity is part of that plan.

If the devil exists, I think we're already lovers.

Don't fault us for hiding our hurt better than you—by being 'successful', funny or high—we've had more practice.

Don't believe (if you're even reading this) that I'm writing this for you.

You mattered, once, before your kind became a trail of cobblestones to skip across on our way to elsewhere.

Sometimes when the news warn of a impending terrorist attack ('Not *if* but *when*,' I keep hearing), I mentally mail them a list of addresses that they can target.

Stupid straight people killing stupid straight people: you must admit, that's poetry.

I agree, during such moments, I'm not at my best.

At least I know when I'm shit—when do you know you're shit?

Look at how I'm laughing with you in social situations—you could almost think we're friends!

Keep our friends close and enemies in a blue-black box to be tossed down a chasm along the back of the heart.

If we're unlucky, our hearts become imploded stars—but you'd know nothing about that.

Every relationship is different; the banality of logic that eludes you.

I hope your children grow up queer; I hope they write poems about you.

Please don't have children.

My kindness is directed towards them—these ghosts of future anguish, reaching out for love with stubs for fingers—and never you.

Buddhas on the altar shake their heads.

I don't look at them as I write this.

When I think 'terrorist' or 'murderer', I think of you.

This is inspired by a Facebook page called 'Dear Straight People' that has some of us explaining important things to you, as if you're worth it.

Some of us have murdered ourselves, or have thought about doing so once or twice; too many of us are ill; the rest of us love each other the best we can.

Don't tell us society is doing its best.

Sometimes when our best is insufficient, we die.

Life carries on; there're far more important things—*you* don't get to tell me that.

To those of you proud of being 'bisexual' or 'post-homosexual'— please.

Let me introduce you to friends who are actually bi and post-sexual—but why would I want to do that?

That would mean I wear the hope that you can change, like a rubber band around my scrotum.

That I'm writing about you in these pages only means that I'm fondling a scar where once I cut myself; I'm learning to avoid being cut again.

I look back up at the altar—my partner's altar, not mine; where he has allowed me to position my Buddhas, for my sake.

I barrel down these sentences where your faces meet me like syphilitic chancres.

The man I love looks up from reading the newspapers to reassure me about something.

Or to remind me that we should go downstairs for lunch at the hawker centre, where I'll pretend your kind are not present.

An elderly woman with her husband sits at our table without asking; I want to pour hot tea over her permed head of hair.

But he gives me a look, as if to say: 'You're better than that.'

I'm only better with him—or when you're no longer there.

In every X-Men movie that we've watched together, I root for Magneto.

Life is still too short to be better than this.

When I allow myself to be 'better', our skins meet your casual knives.

All of you and your 'good intentions'.

So invite me to your parties again, why don't you—you won't even know I'm there.

Remarks on Nothing

Bird

Because I'm dying (who isn't?), I write about nothing. What does this say about me? Such nothing. I saw a bird with a broken leg perched, as if enjoying the sun, on the edge of a drain. Sadness glided through me. I could do nothing for it. Yet I watched—I'm tempted to say 'over'—it, before standing up into a cloud of empty space that could be mistaken for transcendence or quiet ecstasy. But it, too, passed.

∞

They say nothing can mean everything, if we let it. Zero is a number for an absence, but infinity is the complete lack of absence, even as 'complete' is clearly a misnomer when nothing is complete with infinity, even as a fleeting concept (if you truly think about it: $\infty - 1 = \infty$, still.) If infinity is without bounds, including every absence in its diapason—for every cranny of a one-sided perspective, there are surfaces we fail to explore; cracks on the other side of surfaces and cracks underneath those cracks. If everything is possible, then nothing is possible—and nothing we may return to. Not nothing-as-despair or resignation, not nothing-as-the-opposite-of-some-thing but closer to nothing-as-infinity-if-you'd-only-let-the-brain-shut-up.

You

I keep saying this: one of us will hold the other's hand, it's true, at that moment when we think farewells are the final curtain call. But that's not what I'm harping on; grief is one thing, but nothing is quite another, or it involves grief but not in the way we expect. Expectation is something: thought, the past, hope—no, I mean, nothing is nothing that will envelop us, towards the tapering end. You'd have your gods to consider, your Moksha, lives after this life. I'll have nothing: now-as-nothing; no time at all, dropping your hand with nothing in my head, uninvited, in the same way sorrow will return, but briefly, before receding and nothing is there, or here, once more, an infinite shoreline: the sea not pulling away to sculpt a tsunami—the ocean, really, finally drying up.

Vibrato

A birdcall I mistake for warm vibrato, a soprano warming up
becoming the koel I recognize but shrink from recognizing, because
I want not to break the surface of sound with my discrimination
of that sound; acknowledging instead that surface is singular,
stretching from koel to these ears then my skull, travelling along
the underside of skin to inspire goosebumps, the thrill of an alto
trill beginning in my own throat; an unending surface of vibration,
perhaps, that merges with the vibration of cells in my body, going
deeper still—but what's deeper than the wavering surface of
everything? (Nothing.)

Fairness

Not the senses, not the maelstrom of discrimination and discern-
ment, but farther back towards the wellspring of consciousness
from which reason is wrested and lauded—mind as nothing,
choicelessness, freedom. I must confess (please forgive me) that
such clarity means more to me than whether I love you enough.
But out of nothing, the only truth arising that I favour is love and
the end point of its energy is you. To be fair, I'm an extremist: 'If it
doesn't last, then it wasn't love in the first place.' To be fair: 'I'll only
love you when you love me.'

Feng Shui

How beauty, as we come to know it, is shaped by our circumstances is something men (gay men even more so, I'd argue) are more likely to forget than women. What does this mean for our sense of self? Self-belief is so overrated we don't register that what we feel we feel against our will when we desire or love. Even as we recognize the cliché in this, we remain subjugated by circumstance nonetheless. Knowing or seeing clearly is not freedom, not at first.

Other things shape us—our moods, our capacity for intelligent thought, our actions—and not as a result of when we perceive ourselves as pilots in cockpits, calling every shot. Move a chair here, unfold a screen there, paint three lines overhead, wear more blues or reds, remove plants, place a bowl of water in the corner: create the conditions for a better life, a more beautiful mind. Not that there is no autonomy whatsoever, but where does it end and the pinball machinations of circumstance begin?

Then even when we're happy, is it our happiness (neural alignments, dopamine production, serotonin levels) that speaks or is it *us*? Since nothing we feel or do may be because of us, then everything can be manipulated to grant us what we need. So call our feng shui specialist today, so we can be cleverer, happier, more in love, healthier, etc. Or do nothing and just watch as everything falls apart or comes together—watch without judging ourselves or the circumstances that will ultimately pack our bodies into neat little boxes and tilt us into the crematory fire.

Pain

During my second herniated disc ('All before the age of forty,' the doctor you recommended shaking his head as he reminded me), I didn't just feel stabbed in the back, I was electrocuted by agony. Spasms lasted for minutes that seemed like hours, ensuring I could only sit or lie on one side of my body, quaking helplessly for the twentieth time in the middle of the night (a fish flapping on land, the image I had in mind) and nearly blacking out before I realized I was reaching the limit of how much pain a body can endure, before tottering on the threshold of void. A voice inside me shot out into the darkness: 'Is this all you've got in your arsenal? Is this all?'

In-between moments of calm, and later when I recovered, I still understood that the absence of pain was a deception to be enjoyed ironically, with a mental sneer. I know better now, as death itself might be that final shattering blow I'll meet with gritted teeth. I'll accept this with the fullness of nothing in my mind (pain is pain, neither terrible nor sad) and maybe with an echo of that defiant laughing voice inside my head: 'Is this all you've got? Is this all?'

Poem

A student from Bedok North Secondary School asked during a writing workshop: 'What first inspired you to become a poet?' 'Loneliness,' I replied. I wrote as if my poems were letters to somebody who'd rescue me from a tragic form of solitude. Now I write because I know I've always been alone with myself. The best listener has been my own mind, a private conversation playing out across language towards a resolution of silence and heightened sensitivity. This means that I can still watch and kiss and love you but from inside an aquarium of utter stillness in which I'm floating; until the *I* dissolves and no more poems can be written.

Poet

A fictionist called the poet a choo-choo train that took you along for a ride in a private circle of hell, if you weren't careful. A younger poet engaged with him for hours on WhatsApp, frustrating herself in failing to make him see that he wasn't the person he thought he was, the one most deserving of pity. He was a man of privilege suffering from 'margin envy' (she coined this). His problems had to be greater than yours. He wasn't the only one like this, unfortunately.

I entered the scene because I hoped to find an older poet as a mentor or model of enlightenment, but came across no such person. Everyone was marginalized and misunderstood—a martyr in their romantic narratives of selfhood. 'These are artists and poets I never want to be when I *grow up*,' I told a friend.

Writing has become my own teacher, clearing the weeds of both doubt and understanding so I might stand alone in the garden of nothingness like the first human on a brand-new planet, gracefully stripped of every intention to conquer or be heard (except by the silence inside my skull).

Affair

(I cheat on you in this one.) My boyfriend is a solo salsa dancer on a cruise ship. He's trying to win a competition but he keeps sliding to my table from the dance floor—sweaty, winking and restless—to flirt with me. I love him like how I love you. Then get this: I *know* I'm dreaming and must return to your bedside. But I'm here, and this dream has to end correctly; I must continue being in love and happy in this dream with him. For him. Because nothing is for real, apparently. Every life of love is still a dream. The dream is cut short: I wake up to pee. Nothing is real.

Routine

Sometimes routine gets in the way of nothing. Beginnings are born from nothing and older than endings, since nothing is outside of time. When nothing takes over, the past is anyone's past. Then remembrances lurch behind old habits and nothing is forgotten again. The brain must be trained to let nothing in and its windows left open to air out these many rooms. Sometimes nothing gets in the way of nothing too.

Price

Whitney Houston tells Oprah Winfrey in an interview that she could have lost the spirit to sing. It might seem racist to say this, but I think Houston's voice was black-gold, a tonal cave of shadows and hidden treasure I lost myself in when I first heard 'Miracle' on the radio. But my favourite is Leontyne Price's voice: infinite shades of black; a black rainbow or sometimes black lightning. In her final performance of *Aida*, her sound has lost much of its density, but those pure black notes at the top bring to mind what she recalled from working with the conductor, Herbert von Karajan, in that as a singer, she felt like she had floated into space.

Nothing as blackness; as a clearing of all decks in the mind through resonance; tidal vibration; dark matter. She is my queen of the night. When she waits for the applause to subside after 'O patria mia' ('Oh, my dear country,' for Aida might never see her homeland again), Price is a reed in a howling thunderstorm of adoration—the dignity of her attempt not to cry, to step completely out of character, even though this is the last Aida she will ever inhabit on stage. The humility. That grace. Her eyes are wet full moons, black puddles, open mouths with absolutely nothing more to say.

Equivalences

Nothing=Bluish white light I imagine waiting to be discovered, peeking behind every object, body part, even the skin of ordinary light itself, if I look hard enough or remember to look=Change= Impermanence as afterglow=Everything we feel in relation to the unknown=Threshold=Origin without end=Not detachment, a word that leads to its own attachment; but not over-attachment, too=An easy bag to fill again, but even harder to unfill once more=Released, not releasing=Freshly alive after private ablutions, how even this will be over=No credit claimed, but once seen impossible to unsee=A beautiful soundtrack=Instants when I let go of that which I thought I could never relinquish=Clarity=Behind closed eyes, the darkness with its spots and welts shimmers with a light of its own=At rest, a sensitivity=Not caring any more about this and that, but doing them and caring anyway because since I'm here=One Diwali when I was so exhausted that I closed my eyes without falling asleep while everybody was talking in the living room and I heard everything but didn't react because to do so from one's conditioning is a choice I didn't have to make=People sicken me; I sicken me=Every act of avoidance when (uncountable) others refuse to acknowledge my queerness, my *difference*, manifested by the lack of expression, an *indifference*, which is practised (not always successful) stoicism= With every perspective waiting to compete with each other, why compete at all, or for too long=Unfixing fixities of ideation=More vital to brave countless possibilities than to impose perfection=To settle what is right in front of you/me with neither the wish to blame nor prescribe a comfortable narrative='But the self is always there, right?' 'Nobody is saying there's no self, but why be attached to it?'=Behind one mental wall of prejudice, yearning and habitual responses, lies another wall and further behind this wall=The mirror when we leave the room, but not before we embrace to form a two-faced Janus in the glass=Untroubled autotelicism=Blue light I'm almost convinced is love as nothingness-in-action; light that caresses the underside of shadows=Then when such light is no longer as I imagine it, when hope is the closing track on the album=Infinity

Vakkali Refractions

Inspired by an essay by Stewart Dorward

Thus have I heard.

Almost all scriptures in the Pali canon open with such words (roughly translated here). Some suggest that they refer to how the sutta is more 'hearsay' than anything heard directly from the Buddha. Others say it's a matter of rhetorical convention, a distancing of 'I' from the account, signifying the non-absolutism of both selfhood and all dhamma. (I prefer how this suggests that the story might or mightn't have occurred, at least not in the way it's being told; its ambiguity insisting that we take it both lightly and seriously—not so much as historical record but as an invitation to gentle analysis, even insight—like how it haunts me now.)

The Siddhārtha Gautama, also known as the Blessed One, heard that Venerable Vakkali was unwell. Vakkali later saw the Blessed One coming and stirred in his bed.

I think you can see why this story enthralls me (I know you don't think much about Buddhism when, for you, Hinduism is far more embracive.) Vakkali's 'stirring' sinks its teeth into me. Is this blasphemy? I mean, if I believe Vakkali was queer?

(Of course, queerness was not understood in the same way during that time. But if you think homoeroticism is profane, what does this say about you?)

In one translated version, Vakkali had been attracted to the Buddha's teachings; united, through his eyes, to the Buddha's physical form. At the Sangha, Vakkali followed his teacher around to watch the Blessed One's body. The Buddha commanded Vakkali to leave on account of this. Vakkali was so sad he tried to leap off a mountain. The Blessed One intervened, whispered some verses, and Vakkali walked on air.

Why did the Buddha ask him to leave? Homophobia (whatever that looked like)? Probably not, I wish. Probably that he saw 'leaving' as a transition in the direction of Vakkali's future transcendence (attachment to literal beauty being necessary in order for this monk to surpass it). I like to think so. Anything is possible.

(When Vakkali hears the Buddha's voice on the precipice, I'm reminded of how my own voice returns to me, renewed, both stranger and lover, only when I'm singing beside you in your car—I used to enjoy singing in public; not any more, since my broken voice has grown too *familiar*—with my hand in your lap; a voice from elsewhere, fuller when mingled with the tonality of your attention—or riding it like a wave.)

According to the Theragāthā, Vakkali didn't try to kill himself on Gijjhakūta. After his dismissal, he had tried to calm himself on its slopes, but was too emotional to meditate.

Can you blame queers for being 'too emotional'? Even when we pretend to surf the centrifugal whirlpool of our feelings, is it so hard to realize that the *success* of our pretence is derived from how much we know (consciously or otherwise) that we have failed our society, or how much its heterosexist culture has failed us?

Somebody writes that the Blessed One appeared, stretched out his hand and said, 'Come, monk.' Ecstatic Vakkali floated into space.

Nobody speaks about the tenderness that I recognize in the Buddha's (telepathic) voice, his enticement to elevation like a call to arousal; his ethereal hand like a hand in marriage.

(I take off into nothingness, too, when I'm singing beside you, your listening its own kind of bidding.

Or I'm never more myself during such moments in your car: rising, arising— your silence is my air.)

When Vakkali yearned for the Buddha, the Blessed One arrived and told him: 'Enough, Vakkali, do not stir on your bed. These seats are available, I will sit here.'

Don't overreact. Be still. Don't cling (too much; or to the point of total distortion of all reason.) Good health is impermanent. Desire is impermanent.

Yet why be ashamed of it? If craving brings us suffering, why shouldn't we enjoy the edge of our unhappiness?

More accurately, if the pain transcends us and not vice versa, why not savour it anyway, knowing that we could be abandoned on an island of serenity?

I love this moment when the Buddha sits before his disciple, the space between them filling with love and serenity (flowing from one end), blending and merging with hope and the pain of yearning (from the other).

What is transcendence when there is nothing to transcend?

'For a long time, venerable sir, I have wanted to come see you, but I haven't been fit enough,' Vakkali confessed.

Why 'unfit'? Not just the state of physical health that Vakkali refers to, I like to think. We spend our queer little lives thinking we must be unfit (when we realize we don't belong.)

I know now that the real sickness is in thinking that we were ever incomplete.

The Blessed One replied: 'Enough, Vakkali! Why do you want to see this foul body? One who sees the Dhamma sees me; one who sees me sees the Dhamma.' (In another translation: '... this stinking, rotten body.' In another: '... this vile body.')

The body might be 'vile' but it's not separate from the order of infinity. With one, you perceive the other. Not a trick of the light, but a paradoxical double-image we *see* not with our eyes but the widening socket of the mind.

After a time, bhikkhus approached the Blessed One to deliver news about the end of Vakkali. The Blessed One addressed them: 'Come, bhikkhus, then let us go to the Isigili Slope, where the

Suicide is a topic that makes many Buddhist monks uncomfortable. There are commentaries that make no comment about Vakkali 'using the knife' as being a euphemism for taking one's own life.

clansman Vakkali has used the knife.'

Another commentary adds that Vakkali was conceited in thinking he might rid himself of suffering through suicide; however, the knife caused him such pain that he realized his present state of puthujjana (the cycle of worldly fetters) and, exerting great effort (presumably, meditative analysis), entered arahantship (perfection).

Suicide is acceptable if performed with the right intentions, goes one form of reasoning. Suicide is *always* unacceptable—this other reasoning is probably more sweeping, less rational and (hence, perhaps) more pervasive.

Being uncomfortable with suicide is still an attachment to the notion that physicality is worth preserving (past the point of reason).

If everything is a dream, why not enjoy the dream before we leave it? In deciding to leave the cliff and reach for that invisible hand that lifts you into air, who is anyone else (other than the people you love) to judge (as if they really cared)?

And would it be so wrong to kiss the ground and caress the cliff's jagged edge (in gratitude) before taking that first step into nothingness?

It remains unclear to me, in the end, whether Vakkali died of illness or by his own hand. In any case, queer suicides have been commonplace and can never be fully understood.

'Have you any doubts, Vakkali? Have you any cause for regret?'

'Indeed, Lord, I have many doubts, much cause for regret.'

'Have you nothing to reproach yourself about as regards morals?'

'No, nothing to reproach myself about as regards morals.'

In one translation, this almost-rapid-fire conversation between the Buddha and Vakkali (before the latter reveals that his only pre-death worry is not being able to *see* his teacher) fascinates me for its possible ambivalences; they remain unresolved past the narrative's conclusion, in spite of the storyteller's and the translator's best intentions. In my reading, doubt dwindles like a shadow across the floor of a moment

about whether Vakkali can fully
relinquish his sense of self-hatred.

The body might be foul, but I'd still love
to see you/yours till the end.

The Buddha didn't actually have to
come to Vakkali's bedside. Not coming
to see him could have been a Zen-
lesson in itself; a long-distance missive
bearing a challenge to attain insight.

But the Blessed One came. Imagine
that.

If morality is a dream, a vapour arising
from a steaming bog of conditions and
circumstances. If beauty is a dream.

Somebody recounts the Buddha's
last words as thus: 'All conditioned
things are impermanent. Strive on
with diligence.'

This is my favourite version of the end, in which the Blessed One distantly saw Vakkali in his bed with his shoulder turned away. He also saw smoke, an accompanying darkness, sliding to the east, then spreading in all directions. He then addressed his disciples: 'Do you see, bhikkhus, that cloud of smoke, that darkness?'

'Yes, venerable one.'
'That is Mara, the Evil One, searching for the consciousness of our Vakkali, wondering: "Where now has the consciousness of Vakkali gone?" But know this, dear bhikkhus, with consciousness unestablished, our Vakkali has attained final Nibbāna.'

Mara, Buddhism's Lucifer (another misunderstood angel)—the darkness in every religious story painted with light—without whom there would be no understanding of non-duality. The Mara of conditioning and endless craving. It's not craving that is the problem but the inability to appreciate that what we crave is already changing as we speak; the body of the one you love is not just a body but an ever-shifting encounter between a fundamental uncertainty and your still-rewarding idealization of presence (knowing this, what is there not to enjoy, albeit briefly?)

Love our bodies and where they take us.

Kiss the finger, even when it is pointing at the moon.

Vakkali is our metaphor for that homo-
erotic struggle with physical beauty and
its transience. We are Vakkali.

Beauty is in the details—in many
accounts, the Buddha had a beautiful
body. Even in old age, deterioration can
also be beautiful. Even suicide (dare you
imagine this). What is meditation but
an expansion of our imagination, a
semantic widening, the opening of
every window in the room of a word so
the warm night of darkness can blow
straight through?

Blink

Televisions huddle in the Milky Way
but they've missed the train
that circles the multiverse.

Planetary rotation of a sweet in your mouth
is what you know of time.

Trees don't like it
when people discuss their future.
Same for the stars.

What possibility is worth projecting
from our island of forgetting?

Let me go first: such truths
rest better beside the dead.

Your belly undulates, oceans out
like love in every direction.
Everything is possible,

even life without me
or you. But here we are.

After meditating for long enough,
every wall is a craggy cheek
I soothe with thumb or middle finger.

I'm tired of the carpet you bought
to hold up the table.

You're tired of my poems
where I say things I do and don't mean.

Heady world, importunate sky,
openhearted moon.
What you cannot see or say

I only imagine
is real to me. Is real.

Death is a friend.
Sorrow, too.
Impermanence is my truest name.

The weather fights itself:
blazing heat or rain, rain, rain.

All this talk of nothing is making me crazy.
Watch me hide it so you'd never know.

That Pound quote
too often quoted
about making it new.

When the small-mindedness of others
balloons up against my impatience—

their prejudices and indifference—
I want to put a pin right through them
so they collapse to form mounds

of intestinal gore (I know
you wouldn't approve, even though

you know they wish us dead)—
is this new enough for you?

(Insert random line from Hollywood drama
here.) What invades the mind
when the coast is clear.

When televisions on both sides of the corridor
wait to take me to see their families;

their infighting and noisy silences.
The corridor widens them away. No need
to fill time when time doesn't need filling.

To permit only you
to fill the moment, or narrow it

to rooms of your body,
to episodes of our own kind of nothing.

Safewords or points of return:
Gently
It's all there

Don't lose yourself to moments
Return to what marries them

The meditator isn't here right now
Keep watch
Don't lose yourself

Boatless stream without start or finish
How long can you keep this up

Without stopping
Gently

What is new
must also be unexpected
and not what we think

is *new*—
car crash, stalled lift juddering,

bed of thumb slit open, blood
the surprise that keeps on giving—
or else there is no freedom

from our conditioning:
your body too heavy on mine;

your kiss
the same old kiss.

'But surely there must be
a higher power . . .'
But why higher

and lower?
Why the separation?

Energy that is also time.
Cause as effect. Everything
the same power.

The never-ending balancing act
that constitutes us.

This meeting of our hands
becomes a story of their parting.

At a luncheon with Marjorie Perloff,
she tried to persuade me to dislike Sharon Olds'
poetry for its lack of proper lineation.

If even the most intelligent and sensitive
among us cannot accept that absolute universality

is a lie—how a homeless person can find truth
in a speck on the pavement,
incomprehensible to nobody but herself—

only means that subjectivity remains unacceptable;
only means I'm glad to hide

inside the cave of our embrace, separate
from the overreaching insanity of the world.

Ben Lerner writes in *The Hatred of Poetry*,
'Everybody can write a poem,' and asks if
'the distillation of your innermost being . . .

[can] make a readership, however small, a People . . . ?'
Maybe because I'm not American

or because I was never a Universalist,
I've always thought, 'Of course not!'
I write for you (as you watch your action movie

beside me on a plane drifting through turbulence)
but more likely for me—or the infinity within me/us

that doesn't toss, swell or shrink beyond
the vicissitudes of self, the words we tell ourselves.

What is the word that means
an existence of looking
both inwardly—without judgement

or desire to derive absolute sense—
towards an unfolding profundity,

and outwardly from somewhere
beneath the surface of our bodies
at every word, gesture and

reciprocity passing for time, all
without feeling divided, absent,

sorrowful or benumbed?
(Meditation.)

Poets come closer to describing the void precisely.
Novels are televisions that never stop talking.
Televisions are stars rooted in the shock

of their afterglow, while spacetime whirls
and rubs up against them. Stars are hard

of hearing. Stories, too. So caught up
in the drama of mistakes, they demand
to be remanded to the lower courts

of collective amnesia. The lowest court
welcomes Death, the Chief Justice presiding.

We stand trial, but won't be testifying.
Our silence is a poem that dances us to forever.

Nugatory Analysis

The warm, damp, Indian smell of you
this morning; I love the tropic racism
of my fetishism come true
when I wake up to you. Bird call
assuages nothing when it recalls us
back into our room; you barely awake,
but my eyes snapped open
like umbrellas in a thunderstorm
that hasn't happened yet. The window
breathes light in cooling layers
across our skin. I remember to touch
your body under your frayed sleep-
shirt that seems to glow whiter
the longer I lie here, the longer
I know you. I'm so afraid of losing you.

And you're so afraid of losing me:
you mumble as you turn and coo,
our legs clashing, then overlapping;
entangling like roots at the base of a tree.
All this talk of change and departure
inside my poems, inside my head,
that you never realize, that I never let on,
except when you read this now.

Look at how a poem anticipates
the future, the art of hope in the torque
of a line: your eyes turning around
every break and image before abandoning
language to re-enter the real dream
of skin, moistened lip and pliable fingers
on our bed that will one day be empty
of us. No time like the present
is no time at all. How far we've come
that we may understand this. How lucky.

False Labours:
Eight Immortals Passing Through

Knuckles on chest, leg under heftier leg:
how we get trapped under and cannot move.

I seem to weigh less every morning.
My tibia is Han Xiangzi's flute

whittled from golden bamboo
and played with a broken heart; his lover

imprisoned by her father at the bottom
of an ocean. My bones are hollow music.

That owl-hoot of an old woman
breathing beats during qigong

is He Xiangu between gulps of vomit
discharged by mendicants; suffering

without suffering at the hands of her mistress.
A meme of a baby swaddled by a mother's shirt

and calming down mightn't be about love
but about the bliss of repetition:

tenderness for what feels like nothing new.
Lan Caihe floats between genders over a basket

of flowers down a river of flux, a shoe
fallen off. Neither young nor old. Perpetual

child on the inside. Spirituality is a state
of mind as timeless, selfless affection.

You tell me how Sufis danced, rooted to the source.
My fingers do the flamenco across your waist.

After riding for a thousand li, Zhang Guolao
folds his donkey into a box or one of his pockets.

He declined invitations from emperors. I sit
all day at home beside you, staring into space.

Han Zhongli is like Budai with a fan,
fanning stones into gold and into stones again.

I imagine poems are pebbles in my skull
unloaded onto these pages, where they become

pebbles of gold. Lü Dongbin, multi-hyphenate—
poet-drinker-swordsman-seducer—could be

Guanyin re-animated, re-emanated. I'm not
handsome like him, but I'm your baby in the dark.

Together, the dim shape our bodies make is protean:
bag of rocks, mountainous terrain, discrete forms again.

In daylight, I remember you as ex-civil servant
but with only a towel to wrap your nakedness

before your gods on the altar, rudraksha beads
dripping from your wrist; covert prayers

chasing each other across your lips. What you
remind me of on a dry-iced stage inside my head:

Cao Guojiu in officious robes, even as an immortal;
after handing his riches to the poor for a brother's sins.

Giving everything and gaining more than everything
in return. The stories the same: everyone flew

post-hermitage and upon private cultivation;
once realizing that what they had to give up

was nothing at all. Truth as practice as awareness
as heavenward departure from cloudy conditioning.

I'm keen to fly beyond flying, like Tieguai Li;
suffering temptation, reborn disabled, a tramp.

(Are you surprised I relate to him most of all?)
Squatting quietly, irascible, mincing feelings

under a tree (I assume) before this recognition:
'All is farce, fuss-free, appearances, nothing

more.' Your stomach as resting gourd—replete
with medicinal serenity. Our life together

an iron clutch or vaulting pole I employed for lift-
off from shaky ground; hobbling free

of freedom, self, emotional fixities. Eight
immortals as eight-for-infinity; perhaps, Sufi-like

circularity. No more effort beyond love
without labour. How far from you I've been taken

towards Elysium without ever having moved at all.

Swimming Lessons

My answer to that mirror above the sink
is still, *No*.

Every pleasure negligible,
every discomfort
like Rothko to the sightless.

Failure to leave
your favourite room of a house
in flames;

or restlessly engaged
like a Gemini (seldom still).

In a scroll painting,
another stupid parakeet
strains its gaping beak
towards another stupid peach.

Base time.
Forward time.
No time.

If I love you,
nothing in my body
is loving you; but, yes,
I still call it love.

My reflection in the glass
is a window
inside another window.

If engrams chart different pathways
through the brain each time we remember;
if recollection is closer to reconstitution
than replication—

what is this past we cling to
like nails to a plank.

This isn't a lesson in profundity.

Let's not marry death to beauty.

Watching without thinking
that we're watching
without thinking.

Knowing without pre-knowledge
or future accumulation—

Yet when I forget my keys,
the names of previous lovers—

Some things might be worth remembering.

Small things.
Soft
or hard things,
like stones in a pocket
Woolf carried into the River Ouse.

At the end of breathing, the heart
beats the body
into submission,
demanding life; more and more life.

When what demands
isn't the self
demanding exactly
but the undertow of circumstance and habit.

Sometimes
memory
is a hypnotist.

Sleepwalk.
Sleep
talk.
Final, unending sleep.

Or no real sleep at all; neither now
nor even (some say) in the hereafter.

Practice makes perfect;
practice without practising.

Start. Re-
start.
Gently

watch whales
of expectation
surface
then sink
without a splash of commentary.

Surface.
Sink.
Swim.

No answers to reflections.
No lesser answer to mirrors of the mind.

Light glancing off the ocean;
a dancer across its wild, uninterrupted back.

A dancer in pieces—

Sun-shards
as uncollected,
half-forgotten truths.

The farther forest monks
retreat, the more they're sought after
by those who've found no solace
in dismembering the ego and being
totally still.

Beginning of the end;
the beginning
is the end.

Last few minutes of Tarkovsky's *Solaris*:
foggy, encircling waves of an alien planet
hewing to a traveller's
longing and regret—he buckles

to his knees before the father he abandoned
to embrace him
forever; forgetting
how even inside their reconstructed house,
the ceiling wept smoky tears.

No delusion too distant from the truth.
No man unmarked by another.
Nothing separate from everything.

Not forgetting the fog
from which reality is obsessively fashioned.
(I must learn to unmake its fabric.)

Not forgetting those waves rippling
like shattered mouths
that widen in every direction;
as the camera zooms out
like the eye of an all-powerful deity
with something else better to do—

Don't kid
but save
yourself: abandon
ship. Time

(without which the self
disappears) is smoke and mirrors
and carnivorous waters.

If we're loving and good,
it's because we're loving and good.
(Assign credit only where credit is due.)

In a daydream, I'm lost
in Aokigahara, Suicide Forest or Sea
of Trees, northwest of Mount Fuji, and alone
without you.

I don't want to die.
I don't want to live

but I'm dying nonetheless from being
stranded without food and water;
my stomach cramping; gnarled trees
spreading over my head, cracking all their knuckles.
Losing consciousness, I memorize a sky
rent (*in pieces*) by those branches,
a chill sewn to my bones—

. . . *yet what is the body?* I repeat,
even in this fantasy of death.
A concatenation of sensations; ever-shifting hues . . .

Then I'm awake. (When a corpse
drops in a dream, does it make a sound

worth recording?)
And what is the purpose
of such records?

Poetry: sorting of my mind—

smoke, trees, mirrors,
the sea rippling in every direction—

and a meditation, which has nothing
to do with feeling good.

I've a friend who doesn't know
she's addicted to dopamine spikes in her brain
each time she reconstructs her memories
to preserve a family legacy

entirely imagined:
when relatives she meets
meet the profiles she has devised for them,
the anticipation of meeting them
makes her happy.

Then when they disappoint,
she reformulates elaborate justifications around them
so the process towards anticipation is repeated.

Same with another friend and his gorgeous cat.

Same with me and you, whenever you
climb into our bed with that grin on your face.

When you accuse me of staying unhappy
in spite of all you've done for us,
there's nothing more I may say beyond
I'm neither pleased nor displeased.

Nothing that I haven't felt
deeply. But knowing
is the peripheral country

I occupy without knowing these days.
The closest word I could align myself to is
detached.

Taking each thing as it comes
like a coin tossed down a well
that grants no more wishes.

Not that I don't still get pissed off:
I want to be that demon-clown in Stephen King's *It*
and rise out from toilet drains in megachurches
or fill out their giant television screens to declaim
(stealing a line from Rowan Atkinson):
'I've come to save you; I'm afraid the Jews were right!'

Or: *Give me gore in my heart,*
keep me burning. Give me gore
in my heart, I pray, I pray . . .

I make myself laugh; some days
there's nothing else.

Most days: there's you
and there's infinity, a bottomless aquarium
I bob in and out of
like a hungry fish.

Or you're a wormhole:
a door that opens into a galaxy
I could visit at any time.

Then when one door closes—

Or when time swings its axe at the door—

By Christmas

I'd like to be gone by Christmas.
Not due to sadness (nothing
so trivial, even as she waves to me
across time) but because I'm done.
Or because I've no more
agenda, nobody left to impress,
nothing to do that somebody
else cannot do, regardless
of what the sitcoms tell me.
Not that life is no longer
hilarious, but such a space
is opening around my tears
and laughter that I'm no longer
certain if I'm myself or the sky.
So bring it on, dear body
(don't expect *me* to do the work):
the casual aneurysm,
pneumonia or multiplication
of cells—what difference
does it make when change
is never new? Not even
that I've stopped caring—
but if my tea leaves inform me
I'm through, I'd nod at the news.

Hell is other people: oh boo-
bloody-hoo. But more likely
that I'll awake next year
beside you; I'd wash the toilet,
teach, read or write
a poem about us again too.
Just in case, let me say goodbye
before it's all over; for in spite
of what anybody says,
I'll always love you.

Acknowledgements

Sections of this collection have appeared in *Ambit*, *The Arkansas International*, *Transnational Literature*, *The Cortland Review*, *Drunken Boat*, *Cordite*, *Pressure Gauge Journal*, *Petrichor*, *Alluvium*, *August Man*, *Truck*, *Hayden's Ferry Review*, *Mascara Literary Review*, *Cha*, *Re-Markings* and *SG Poems 2017–2018*. Mr Kwok, the owner of Sultana Bookstore in Singapore, provided the final quote from Bonny Hicks ('How glorious . . . the word').

You and infinity:
lovers I get caught
in-between. Waking
to your kiss reminds
me again that both
are the same. And how
without one, I'm still
left with the other.